Men-at-Arms • 436

# The Scandinavian Baltic Crusades 1100–1500

D Lindholm & D Nicolle · Illustrated by A McBride

*Series editor* Martin Windrow

First published in Great Britain in 2007 by Osprey Publishing,
Midland House, West Way, Botley, Oxford OX2 0PH, UK
44-02 23rd St, Suite 219, Long Island City, NY 11101, USA
Email: info@ospreypublishing.com

Osprey Publishing is part of the Osprey Group.

Transferred to digital print on demand 2011

First published 2007
5th impression 2010

Printed and bound by PrintOnDemand-Worldwide.com, Peterborough, UK

A CIP catalogue record for this book is available from the British Library

ISBN: 978 1 84176 988 2

Series Editor: Martin Windrow
Page layouts by Alan Hamp
Index by Alan Thatcher
Originated by PPS Grasmere, Leeds, UK
Typeset in Helvetica Neue and ITC New Baskerville

**Artist's note**

Readers may care to note that the original paintings from which the colour plates in this book were prepared are available for
private sale. All reproduction copyright whatsoever is retained by the Publisher. Enquiries should be addressed to:

Scorpio Gallery
PO Box 475
Hailsham
East Sussex
BN27 2SL
UK

The Publishers regret that they can enter into no correspondence upon this matter.

**The Woodland Trust**

Osprey Publishing is supporting the Woodland Trust, the UK's leading woodland conservation charity, by funding the
dedication of trees.

**www.ospreypublishing.com**

# THE SCANDINAVIAN BALTIC CRUSADES 1100–1500

## INTRODUCTION

**M**OST PEOPLE are familiar with the Crusades to the Holy Land during the Middle Ages; others know of the Reconquista, in what are now Spain and Portugal, which was another form of medieval crusade. In contrast, the crusades that took place around the Baltic Sea during the same period are less well known. Even those studies which have been made have emphasized the role of Germans, and above all the Germanic military orders – the Sword Brethren, and the Teutonic Knights – rather than that of the Scandinavian peoples who played such a vital role.

These expeditions were regarded as genuine crusades, both by the medieval European Church and by those who took part in them. The Baltic Crusades, as they are now known, were sanctioned by Papal authority; and they had a profound impact upon the subsequent history of all the states that surround the Baltic Sea.

### Definitions of a crusade

In recent times a 'crusade', in its original religious and warlike sense, has generally been regarded simply as an ugly phenomenon from the Western world's blood-stained past, without much consideration being given to the actual origins of the term. To the Christian peoples of the Middle Ages, however, the word had a very specific meaning: it was an armed expedition or series of expeditions intended to remove a perceived threat to the Christian faith, or to convert non-Christians to Christianity (by force if necessary), or to achieve both these ends.

Not all such religiously inspired armed conflicts were against Muslims or pagans, however. Those against the Albigensians in southern France were undertaken to crush a 'heresy'; while those against the Byzantine Imperial capital of Constantinople, against Bulgars, Hussites and other peoples and communities in Europe, pitted Latin or Catholic Christians against Christians who adhered to a different version of the faith. Meanwhile, the so-called 'Italian Crusades' were little more than political wars to maintain or extend Papal power. At the legal core of all such crusades lay the fact that such military efforts had to be sanctioned by the Pope – Christ's representative on earth – or, at the least, by a respected bishop who was himself representing the Pope.

Participating in a crusade offered many material and spiritual benefits for the believing Western European Christian, and this was as true of the Baltic Crusaders as it was of those who mounted expeditions to the Holy Land in Palestine. These benefits may be summarized as follows:

While a man was on crusade, all his assets were protected; they could not be seized in payment of taxes or other debts. All his sins were

The Danish knight Henrik Plot in full armour, shown in a 14th century stained glass window. This illustrates the transitional styles of body defence – probably with a coat-of-plates worn over a mail hauberk and 'soft' armour – as also found in the grave-pits at Visby. (*in situ* Döllefjelde Church, Denmark)

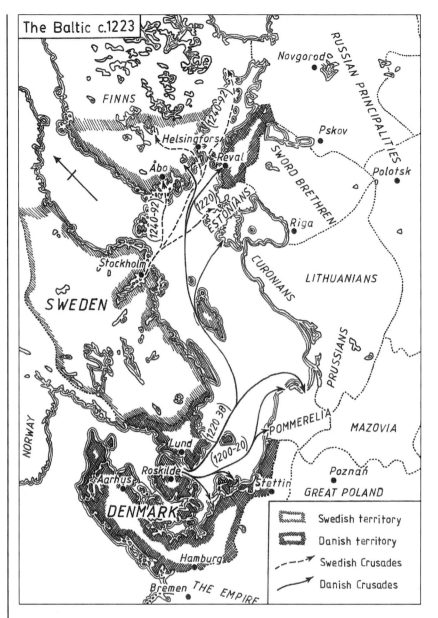

The Baltic c.1223

Legend:
- Swedish territory
- Danish territory
- Swedish Crusades
- Danish Crusades

forgiven, including those committed while on the crusade itself. A crusader would not be prosecuted for any crimes committed before the crusade, and if he fulfilled his oath and completed his crusade (and survived), then these crimes would be forgiven by the worldly authorities; in other words, a man could return home with a clean slate, both spiritually and legally. Any loot that he might take while on crusade could usually be kept, although a tithe was normally expected to be paid to the Church out of such 'profits' of campaigning.

People from all walks of life took part in these ventures, ranging from kings and princes of the blood through every level of society down to the very poorest. Inspired by their faith and their hope for the salvation of their immortal souls, they gathered whatever means they could afford and set off into the distant unknown, to rid the world of those they believed to be 'enemies of the faith'.

In the past, many historians have made much of the fact that the crusades were a means for rulers and communities in times of local peace to rid themselves – at least temporarily – of landless and burdensome younger sons of the propertied classes, and of greedy and troublemaking noblemen whose ambitions threatened the stability of the state. In reality, this does not usually seem to have been the case. Instead, the vast majority of crusaders took part because they believed in what they were doing and accepted what their local religious leaders told them was their duty to God. This was a time when many believed in the teaching of their Church so strongly that they were willing to lay down their lives for it. Difficult as it may be in our secular age, it is essential to grasp these facts if one wishes to understand why the crusades became such a popular movement, drawing in many of the leading political and ecclesiastical princes of Europe to such a remarkable degree.

4

## Participants in the Baltic Crusades

In the early years the Baltic Crusades mostly involved Scandinavia and the German-speaking areas. 'Outremer', or the crusader territories in the Middle East, provided a more appealing arena for southern monarchs and their peoples. After the loss of the last fragments of the Holy Land in 1291, crusading opportunities in the eastern Mediterranean became limited. As a result, French and Burgundian would-be crusaders began to show increasing interest in the pagan lands of the Baltic region, this being especially apparent during the 14th century. The Teutonic Knights, as an international military order of chivalry, could potentially draw upon manpower from right across Christendom, but in reality the Order's recruiting bases were limited to their core lands within the German Empire.

Where the Scandinavian countries were concerned, it was never a very large-scale affair, and there was no question of the Baltic Crusades capturing the imagination of an entire continent in the way that the First Crusade to Jerusalem had done. There were, of course, many volunteers; but for the most part the forces involved were 'royal crusades', carried out by rulers and the retinues that they themselves could muster, whether from Denmark, Norway or Sweden.

The Baltic Crusades, and especially the campaigns directed against the pagan Lithuanians, also came to be seen as offering an opportunity for men to gain valuable military experience without having to travel all the way to the Middle East, where a feeble crusading effort was still under way. It was for these reasons that the Baltic became the most popular region for crusading during the 14th century. This is further highlighted by the fact that the Papal authorities offered the same rewards and conditions to Scandinavian sovereigns as were offered to the English and French when it came to allocating the tax revenues collected by the Church for the specific purpose of financing a crusade. By the mid-14th century the Church came to realize that a dwindling income from these taxes meant that, if continued pressure was to be maintained in the Baltic region, a larger portion needed to be handed over to the monarchs actually involved. Moral pressure was also exerted: for example, St Birgitta of Sweden was at that time extremely influential, both in the Church and in worldly matters. She wrote on the topic of crusading several times, in an attempt to revive interest amongst kings who now seemed to lack sufficient enthusiasm.

The Bishop's Citadel of Kuressare, on the Estonian island of Saaremaa, described as the only medieval fortress in the Baltic States which is virtually complete. Nevertheless, the upper parts of both the walls and the towers were added during the 20th century.

## The Baltic at the time of the Crusades

Since at least the Bronze Age, the Baltic Sea has been a factor which connected rather than divided those peoples and countries which lay around its shores. It provided relatively easy communications and trade routes between many different regions. The fairly modest size and enclosed nature of the Baltic Sea also meant that crossing it was not particularly difficult. During the Iron Age and Early Medieval period – widely known as the Viking period – trade in this region intensified to a remarkable degree. As a result traders and raiders from almost all the surrounding coasts sailed across the Baltic to visit their neighbours, either for peaceful purposes or otherwise.

This had the important effect of ensuring that the peoples of the Baltic Sea possessed much broader and more accurate knowledge of each other than was the case, for example, amongst the early crusaders to the Middle East. In the Mediterranean the coastal and maritime peoples may have known a lot about each other, but the ordinary crusaders from further north and west were woefully ignorant about their Muslim foes.

As the peoples of the Scandinavian Peninsula and of Denmark began to consolidate into kingdoms along essentially Western European lines, the problems posed by tribal raiders from elsewhere in the Baltic ceased to be a local issue which could be dealt with piecemeal. It now became a matter for royal authority and became a state responsibility. It also offered the new rulers of what became Denmark, Sweden and, to a lesser extent, Norway a means of exerting and demonstrating royal power as protectors of their subjects. Although these persistent raids were not the only reason for what subsequently became the Baltic Crusades, they certainly gave added momentum to the movement.

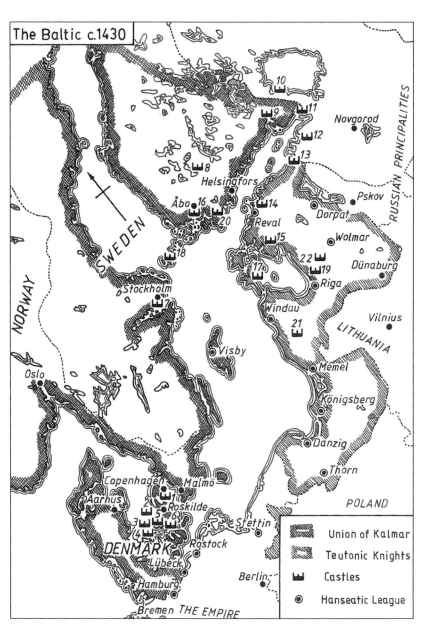

The Baltic c.1430

From the start it became clear that the geographical disposition of the new Scandinavian states enabled them to focus on slightly different regions, at least to begin with. Denmark looked eastward to the Wendish coast of what is now northern Germany, and to the southern or mid-Baltic region of what are now the Polish coast and parts of the new independent Baltic states. Sweden looked towards Finland and the northern parts of the Baltic coastline. To a large extent this disposition also reflected regional politics; Denmark was already much more closely connected by trade and political relationships to northern Germany, while Sweden had closer connections to the rising Russian principality of Novgorod and the tribal areas around Finland.

In considering the following chronology of the major events, readers should bear in mind that the earliest campaigns were not strictly speaking 'crusades', because the Pope had not yet sanctioned them as wars conducted in the name of Christianity. Pope Urban had proclaimed 'the Crusade' (the First Crusade) in 1096, directed towards recapturing the Holy Land from the Muslims. It would take many years before the idea of a 'northern' or Baltic Crusade took root in Scandinavia. However, in 1103 King Eric I 'Ever Good' of Denmark made an armed pilgrimage to Palestine, the first European crowned ruler to visit the newly established Crusader Kingdom of Jerusalem – although he died on his way home. Four years later Sigurd Jorsalafar, one of the co-rulers of Norway, also made an epic voyage from Scandinavia through the Straits of Gibraltar to the eastern Mediterranean, where his little fleet helped the crusaders conquer the coast. This should again, perhaps, be regarded as an armed pilgrimage, since the broader idea of 'crusading' – as a calling, distinct from the specific expedition which we now call, with hindsight, the 'First Crusade' – had not yet fully developed.

# CHRONOLOGY

1095–99  First Crusade to the Holy Land.
1103  Pilgrimage of King Erik of Denmark to the east.
1108  An appeal for help is made in the northern German Diocese of Magdeburg.
1135  Danish attack on the Slav (Rugian) island of Rügen.
1147  The first 'northern crusade' against the pagan Baltic Slavs.
1168–69  King Valdemar I of Denmark attacks and conquers Rügen island.
1171  Pope Alexander III authorizes crusades against the pagan populations of the eastern Baltic (Slav, Balt and Finn tribes).
1185  Pomeranian Slavs surrender to King Canute IV of Denmark.
1188  Estonians (Finns) raid the Swedish city of Uppsala.
1198  Pope Innocent III authorizes the Livonian Crusade against the eastern Baltic coast.
1200  Bishop Albert establishes the see of Riga (now in Latvia) and the Order of Sword Brothers.
1206  Valdemar Seijre leads his fleet against the Osilian (Estonian-Finn) island of Ösel, supported by Archbishop Andreas Sunesen of Lund.

**1200–09** Conquest of the Livs (now central Latvia) by crusaders and Bishop Albert.

**1217** Pope Honorius III authorizes a crusade against the Prussians (now in north-eastern Poland and the Russian enclave of Kaliningrad).

**1219** King Valdemar II of Denmark goes on a crusade against the Ests; according to legend the Danish national flag miraculously fell from the sky at the battle of Lyndanise during this expedition. King Valdemar founds the city of Reval (now Tallinn) and initiates the conquest of northern Estonia.

**1226** German Emperor Frederick II's Bull of Rimini grants Prussia to the Teutonic Order in what are now north-eastern Poland, the Russian enclave of Kaliningrad and part of western Lithuania.

**1230** Pope Gregory IX authorizes the Teutonic Knights to attack the pagan Prussians.

**1231–40** The Teutonic Knights and other German crusaders conquer the western Prussian tribes.

**1236** The German Order of Sword Brothers is virtually wiped out by the pagan Lithuanians at Siaulai (Saule).

**1240** First Baltic Crusade against the Russians of Novgorod; Swedish crusaders defeated by Prince Alexander Nevski.

**1249** Conquest of the central regions of Finland (pagan Sumi and Emi tribes) by Swedish forces under Birger Jarl.

**1254–56** Conquest of the pagan Samogitians in Samland (now the eastern part of the Russian enclave of Kaliningrad).

**1290** Conquest of pagan Semigallia (now coastal Lithuania) by the Teutonic Knights of Livonia (now Latvia).

**1291** Fall of crusader-held Acre in Palestine; transfer of the headquarters of the Teutonic Knights to Venice.

**1292** Swedish crusaders establish an outpost in pagan Korela (Finnic) territory at Viborg (now Vyborg in north-western Russia).

**1300** Swedes fortify Landskrona on the River Neva (now St Petersburg in north-western Russia) on the frontier between the pagan (Finn) Korela and Izhora tribes.

**1308** Teutonic Knights occupy Danzig (now Gdansk in northern Poland).

**1309** The headquarter of the Teutonic Knights is moved from Venice to Marienburg in Prussia (now Malbork in Poland).

**1318** Novgorodians raid Swedish-ruled Finland and burn the cathedral in Åbo (now Turku).

**1323** Treaty of Nöteborg ends the war between Sweden and Novgorod; peace is agreed between the Teutonic Knights and Grand Duke Gediminas of Lithuania.

**1346** King Valdemar IV of Denmark sells Danish-held territory in what is now northern Estonia to the Teutonic Knights.

**1348** King Magnus of Sweden invades Russia (King Magnus' First Crusade).

**1350** King Magnus of Sweden's Second Crusade.

A king and one of his retainers or guards, in a late 12th century Swedish-Danish relief carving. Note that the helmet, right, is of the almost flat-topped form but still has a nasal; the mail coif covers almost the whole face and is shown in a different stylized manner to the mail hauberk. The soldier is otherwise armed with a tall, almost flat-topped kite shield and a sword. (*in situ* Lyngsjö Church, Skåne, Sweden)

1362 Christian Prussians and crusaders capture western Lithuanian city of Kaunas.

1364 Pope Urban V issues a Bull urging a continuation of the crusade against the Duchy of Lithuania, the last 'pagan' state in Europe.

1381 Cannon used by Teutonic Knights for the first time on the River Nemen.

1382 Teutonic Knights seize the Lithuanian capital of Vilnius.

1381 Jogalio (Jagiello) becomes ruler of the still largely pagan Grand Duchy of Lithuania.

1386 Grand Duke Jagiello of Lithuania is baptized as a Christian, is crowned King of Poland as Ladislas II, and founds the Jagiellon dynasty which ruled Poland until 1668.

1398 Teutonic Knights capture the Swedish island of Gotland and regain Samogetia from Grand Duke Alexander Vytautas (Witold) of Lithuania.

1409 Samogetians revolt against Teutonic Knights' rule.

1410 Poles and Lithuanians defeat the Teutonic Order at the battle of Tannenberg.

1423 Last German crusaders reach Prussia.

1429 Teutonic Knights sent to defend Hungary against the Ottoman Turks.

1454–66 The Thirteen Years' War between Poland-Prussian rebel alliance and Teutonic Knights; Teutonic Knights lose western Prussia but retain eastern Prussia as vassals of the Polish crown, and remain independent in Livonia (now Latvia and Estonia).

1496 Swedish forces attack the Russian (Muscovite) fortress of Ivangorod on the eastern frontier of Estonia.

1502 Wolter von Plettenberg, Master of the Teutonic Knights in Livonia, defeats Czar Ivan II of Muscovy at Lake Smolina.

1561 Livonia divided between Poland and Sweden (Ösel island to Denmark in 1573).

# THE ARMIES

In Early Medieval and High Medieval Scandinavia a system of defence was developed which was still largely based on the characteristic Viking Age dependence upon ships. It came to be known as the *ledung*, and it enabled a ruler to summon a specified number of fighting men from a particular geographical region. By the time of the Baltic Crusades each *hundare* district should have been able to muster up one hundred men and four ships, and formed part of a larger region called a *svealand*. The vessel was called a *snäcka* or 'seashell', and was technologically a descendant of the Viking age warship. Meanwhile the *svealand* formed the core of the Swedish kingdom, and could muster as many as 2,200 warriors. There were, in addition, a varying number of volunteers.

The *ledung* was a way of organizing an army to campaign outside its own territory and, as such, proved very useful for Baltic crusading expeditions. This *ledung* had its roots in the Viking Age, and was found in all Scandinavian countries at one time or another. First formalized in Denmark during the first half of the 11th century, it provided a legal method whereby a king could muster an army – or collect taxes paid as an alternative to attending the muster. The concept went back to the 9th and 10th centuries, when 'Sea Kings' could be elected and given provisional authority over men who had assembled for a limited time or to achieve certain limited and pre-agreed goals. Nevertheless, these early and temporary 'kingships' had no power of enforcement over their men, and exercised authority only by consent. Being centred upon a ship, such an organizational unit consisted of the ship itself, the men it carried plus their personal equipment and provisions; all the ship's company agreed to serve for a set number of days.

The *ledung* system of assembling men must not be confused with 'feudalism', since the *ledung* was not gathered around leaders on the basis of their nobility or seniority by birth. Instead it involved free men who owned farms and who were eligible for military duty, and as such it had more in common with later concepts of military conscription. No exemptions from taxation or any other sort of reward were offered as compensation for service; the service itself remained an obligation. On the other hand, the taxes demanded in place of service from those individuals who did not present themselves to serve later became a permanent tax, especially after the *ledung* was abandoned in favour of more truly feudal methods of assembling an army. Although the *ledung* eventually declined, the raising of levies of free men remained an aspect of military power in all Scandinavian countries until the emergence of true conscript armies in the 17th century.[1]

Finland may also have had some form of *ledung* system after its conquest by Sweden, and the *ledung* system was certainly used in Denmark as well as in Norway. At its most basic level the system relied on each *hemman* or farm supplying one armed man, thus spreading the burden of providing adequately equipped footsoldiers throughout the entire community.

The 14th century saw significant changes in the socio-political climate and in military technology, both of which resulted in a different military situation. By now the Scandinavian nobility had also strengthened its ability to muster well-armoured and well-mounted cavalry forces. The evidence shows that a great many, perhaps even a majority of early Baltic Crusaders in the 12th century had been well armed. Subsequently, during the 13th and 14th centuries, mounted troops were raised from amongst the aristocracies of the crusading nations, although foot soldiers still formed the core of armies raised by the *ledung* system, again supplemented by volunteers. In contrast, the knightly military orders had a different organizational and military structure. They represented the only standing forces available for the Baltic Crusades, other than the household troops of the bishops and the settler nobility of the newly conquered territories.

**Inlaid silver decorations from a 12th century sword blade. Although excavated on the eastern side of the Baltic Sea, the weapon was almost certainly made in Germany or Scandinavia; the decorations show warriors in typical 12th century European knightly equipment. (after D.A.Drboglav)**

1 See MAA 399, *Medieval Scandinavian Armies (2) 1300–1500.*

# EQUIPMENT OF THE SCANDINAVIAN CRUSADERS

## ARMOUR & WEAPONS, 1100–1300

When studying medieval military equipment, horse-harness and related objects, we are always faced with the question of how representative the surviving artefacts really are. Where Scandinavia is concerned, it is also important to recognize that, in military as in so many other respects, this region was not quite the same as Continental Europe. An interesting example of this phenomenon was the Norwegian *Kongshird* ('king's army'), a military force which the written sources assure us was well equipped by Scandinavian standards. Nevertheless, the *Kongshird* lacked items such as great helms and plate reinforcements to its armour, at a time when these were widespread amongst the knights of France or Germany. For instance, in the region of Upplsandslagen during the 13th century, the law required that only one man from every *hemman* need achieve the same standard of military equipment that was expected of every man in the *Hird*, which consisted of the king's best men.

RIGHT **Scandinavian inscribed effigial slabs: 12th century knight from Vejerslev in Denmark, believed to be identified as a crusader because of the cross on his helmet and carried in his hand.**

FAR RIGHT **The knight Birger Persson and his wife, 1327. His armour is of the old-fashioned type, consisting of ringmail without plate additions. (*in situ* Uppsala Domkyrka, Uppsala)**

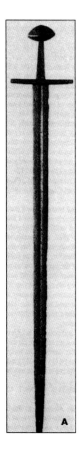
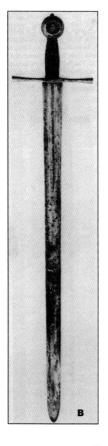

(A) Sword from Denmark, second half of the 12th century (National Museum, Copenhagen; photograph via E.Oakeshott)

(B) Sword from Scandinavia, second half of the 13th century (private collection; photograph via E.Oakeshott)

(C) Sword from Denmark, second half of the 14th century (National Museum, Copenhagen; photograph via E.Oakeshott)

Military demands and the availability of arms and armour differed considerably between the Scandinavian countries. These variations tended to reflect wealth and access to the major arms-producing centres of Western Europe. The standards of military equipment in medieval Denmark were, for example, somewhere between those of the poorer states of Norway and Sweden to the north, and wealthier Germany to the south. Furthermore, much of the Danish aristocracy had close links with the northern German aristocracy, which eased the spread of new ideas and military 'fashions'.

Throughout Scandinavia fighting men used whatever they could obtain or was issued to them by higher authority. Arms, armour and costume were in no sense uniform. Documentary sources might record the level of equipment that was required, as a sort of ideal. Medieval illustrated sources record what an artist thought men should have, based on his own observations and what he learned from pattern books. Whether such written and pictorial evidence reflected current reality is a very different matter.

Scandinavia was not a military backwater, yet the nature of warfare in the Baltic region was not the same as that in France, England, Spain or the Crusader states of the Middle East. Scandinavian armies were relatively small, and local geography reduced the role of heavily armoured cavalrymen – in fact, the terrain in which they operated often rendered their traditional tactics difficult or even redundant. Consequently, foot-soldiers were even more important than they would otherwise have been.

This resulted in various laws or requirements concerning the military equipment of infantry troops. One 13th century Swedish legal codex called the *Upplandslagen* specified that every footsoldier must be equipped with a shield, a sword, a helmet, a mail hauberk or other armour, and a bow with 36 arrows. These requirements were similar to those of a well equipped Viking warrior from a century and a half earlier.

Until well into the 12th century the ordinary infantryman's shield was still round in shape, and the popularity of this form may actually have persisted even longer, since it was both reliable and easy to make. Further developments in the design and structure of shields initially reflected the changing needs of mounted combatants, resulting in an elongated or so-called 'kite' shield which could protect their vulnerable legs. This was then gradually shortened and made more curved in section, which offered greater resilience to blows without adding much weight. Eventually these elongated shields were also adopted by men fighting on foot.

The most typical Scandinavian sword of this period remained the single-hand weapon that had been used since at least the 11th century; this had straight edges, a pommel of round, oval, disc or almond shape, and a straight crossguard. The only real change was in the point, which gradually became more acute, permitting thrusting as well as cutting. While even this was not universal, the evidence nevertheless tends to support the idea that methods of using a sword laid increasing emphasis on the point rather than relying so much on the edge.

Scandinavian helmets from this period included the pointed or conical so-called Norman helmet, with or without a nasal guard. Another type was a variation on this style with a rounded top. It is also possible that, during the 1140s, an older style of Viking Age helmet with eye- and noseguards (usually known as the Gjermundby form) might still have been used. During the 13th century helmets used by mounted combatants reflected Continental European fashions; many if not most were probably imported from Germany or elsewhere. The first such new fashion was for faceguards; these started as simple plates attached to ordinary helmets, but gradually became larger. From this the fully enclosed helmet or great helm soon developed, and was used in Scandinavia as elsewhere in Western Europe, though only by cavalry. By contrast, the broad-brimmed 'kettle' helmet or chapel-de-fer became much more popular in 13th century Scandinavian armies, being cheap to manufacture and highly effective. A distinctively Scandinavian version of this 'war-hat' would in fact be developed during the 14th century.

The most typical body armour was the mail hauberk, usually with each ring having five others passed through it and riveted closed. The mail shirts used during the Viking Age probably did not reach much further than the groin at most, and some were noticeably shorter, while mail sleeves that only reached the elbows were considered adequate. Again, the rising importance of cavalry and their greater need for protection led to significant changes in armour, including mail hauberks that reached to mid-thigh and with wrist-length sleeves; thereafter, mail mittens were added to protect the hands. A later development was mail leggings, supported by a belt or strapped around the rear of the legs. Another development was the mail coif or hooded extension of the hauberk, replacing the earlier mail avential that was sometimes attached to the rims of helmets. The mail hood then developed into a separate piece of armour. All forms of mail were secured to the body or limbs using leather cords, otherwise the mail tended to flap about, making the wearer clumsy, slow and tired.

Two bronze mace-heads, 13th century. This type of weapon was widespread and came in many forms; the simplest version was simply a wooden cudgel with iron studs hammered in. (National Museum, Copenhagen; and Malmö Länsmuseum)

The final item of armour was the gambeson, a form of soft armour. This was not a new invention, the Romans having worn something similar. During the Middle Ages the gambeson underwent several changes but retained its original purpose – to absorb a blunt impact and even to resist piercing attacks. Cloth, when well padded, is superior to metal when absorbing the shock of a blow; when worn beneath mail armour the padded gambeson also protected the wearer from the chafing, winter cold or sun-warmed heat of metallic armour. Sometimes gambesons were worn on their own, as the only armour available to footsoldiers, being relatively cheap to manufacture.

## The importance of the bow and crossbow

Scandinavians had a long tradition of using substantial bows in both hunting and warfare, a simple 'self' bow being used from the Viking Age well into the later medieval period. Their sizes varied from relatively short to what might be called true 'longbows', but whether that term should properly be used is largely a matter of semantics. Long bowshafts have survived from the preceding millennia, for instance from the bogs of Nydam. A wall painting in Södra Råda church includes a figure with a short bow on his left shoulder; one bow found in Norway was 35in (89cm) long, while illustrations from the Viking era also depict weapons that look shorter than what would now be regarded as longbows. All the available medieval evidence points towards the use of bows of a metre or so in length. The documentary sources refer to them simply as 'bows', without further distinction, but the term 'longbow' was an English one that was first used in 1448. It is important to understand that the size of the bow was intended to suit the stature of the individual archer, and to attempt any sophisticated classification from the random survivals is quite unsafe. Most bows in the Baltic region seem to have been made of a single piece of wood, with no evidence of lamination.

Arrows of the bodkin type are known to have been an ancient design, and many have been found in boat-graves dating from the 6th to 9th century Vendel and Valsgärde periods. These narrow or needle-shaped arrowheads facilitated the penetration of armour, of no matter what sort; arrows with broad heads were less suitable in warfare, since they were generally unable to penetrate even ringmail armour.

What is more important was how these simple bows were used. There seem to be no records of bows or crossbows being used in large specialized formations, as would be the case in much of Continental Europe. Perhaps the archers were dispersed amongst other troops, being employed defensively – as was the case in 14th–15th century England. However, the fact that the Upplandslagen military laws stipulated that each *ledung* man should have a bow and arrows suggests that the men were expected to be able to use them. Perhaps archery was something that every man was expected to be able to do reasonably well, but at which very few were specialists – as was often the case in Continental Europe.

The crossbow's importance in Scandinavia and some other parts of the Baltic can be seen from its early appearance, and from the large numbers of crossbow bolts that are almost routinely found at fortifications and battle sites. In fact the crossbow became the weapon of

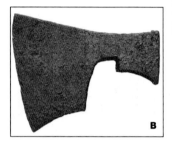

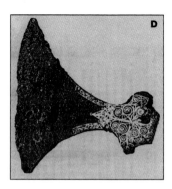

(A) A highly decorated 12th or 13th century sword from Finland, with an inlaid pommel and quillons. (National Museum, Helsinki)

(B) A heavy axe head; this would have been more of a tool than a weapon, but would have been used by peasant warriors if nothing else was available. (Universitets Oldsakssamling, Oslo)

(C) Axehead from Norway, of a type which would have been useful both as a weapon and as a woodsman's axe. This design remained in use with minor changes from the Viking Age to the 18th century. (Universitets Oldsakssamling, Oslo)

(D) A highly decorated 10th to 13th century axe from Finland, the inlaid socket part with front and rear extensions along the sides of the helve. (National Museum, Helsinki)

choice for common soldiers, along with the spear or halberd, and remained so even into the early 16th century period of unrest. The first recorded use of the crossbow by Scandinavians dates from 1170 and the Danish crusade against the Estonians, and its popularity increased steadily thereafter. It was considerably easier to use than a hand bow, and required far less practice to achieve an acceptable level of skill. It shot bolts at greater speed than a bow, resulting in greater damage to the target and being more effective against armour.

The 13th century saw further adoption of the crossbow, which proved to be especially effective in siege warfare, most notably from behind cover inside fortifications. As a consequence the crossbow became an indispensable asset in the hands of Baltic Crusaders. In some respects the simple or early form of crossbow was actually easier to manufacture than a good quality handbow, its bolts or shafts certainly being a lot less sophisticated than a good arrow. The armour-penetrating points used on crossbow bolts remained very similar to those normally used with the hand bow. The most widespread type was a solid bodkin point that could easily puncture mail and, under favourable conditions, could even penetrate plate armour or helmets.

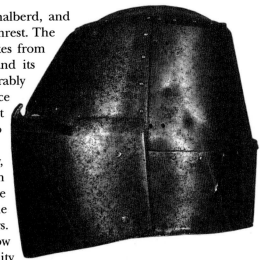

A mid-14th century German great helm, known as the Prank Helm, of a type used throughout those regions influenced by, and supplied with military equipment from, Germany. (Waffensammlung, Vienna; Ministry of Works photograph)

## Close combat weapons

Other weapons that were used during the Baltic Crusades included the war-axe. This came in a variety of types, but the heavy battleaxe was largely fictional: a real war-axe needed to be light enough to wield quickly in order to be an effective weapon. The effectiveness of the axe was largely due to its cutting weight being concentrated at one end of the shaft, rather than being spread out along its length, as with a sword; consequently the total weight of a war-axe could be considerably less than that of a sword. Such war-axes ranged from those held in one hand to those with longer shafts wielded in both hands. The latter, in Scandinavian hands, may actually have influenced the development of pole-arms in Russia.

Two small wooden buckler-type shields believed to date from the 13th century; they are re-inforced with decorative metal strips and with large central bosses over their fist-grips. (National Museum, Copenhagen)

The spear remained a very important weapon, being cheap and straightforward to make and easy to use. When wielded in conjunction with a shield it was also highly effective as the weapon of infantry formations facing mounted enemies. During the 13th century, if not earlier, the mace also became increasingly popular, perhaps primarily in reaction to increasingly heavy armour. The mace can be seen primarily as

an armour-breaking weapon, in contrast to the concentrated cutting or penetrating action of a sword, axe or spear. The distinctive medieval mace had studs, spikes or short, blunt, blade-like flanges for increased impact through the concentration of the whole weight of the blow in small areas of the surface.

The dagger or knife obviously came in many shapes and sizes, since it was an indispensable tool for everyday chores and for eating food. Such an all-purpose utility knife had a blade of about the length of a man's hand, usually with a single edge. By contrast, the dagger or true fighting knife was fashioned primarily as a weapon and was neither intended nor suitable for the cutting of food or other working tasks. Not many examples of true daggers are illustrated in early medieval European or Scandinavian art, and this weapon only came into its own during the later Middle Ages, reaching a peak of popularity in the 15th century.

## ARMOUR & WEAPONS, 1300-1400

The major changes first took place in Continental Europe rather than in Scandinavia during the second half of the 13th and the first half of the 14th centuries, most notably in the addition of plate reinforcements to vulnerable areas of the body and limbs. The earliest such additions were to the elbows, knees and shoulders, plus the shins and arms – areas that were most commonly struck in mounted combat. Consequently it was amongst horsemen that such developments first occurred.

Another more gradual change was the development of rigid or semi-rigid body armour culminating in the coat-of-plates. This form of armour consisted of a flexible covering or base of leather or several layers of cloth, to which plates of steel were riveted, the number and size of which varied a great deal. Several examples were found in the grave-pits at Korsbetningen on the Swedish island of Gotland, having been buried following a battle in 1361. The coat-of-plates was worn over a mail hauberk and quilted soft armour. This combination rendered the combatant's torso virtually invulnerable to anything except powerful missile weapons and the heaviest pole-arms, whereas his arms and legs remained relatively exposed.

The helmet also underwent significant changes during the 14th century, the full or great helm being replaced by other types that had

The iron plates from two coats-of-plates excavated from the grave-pits of the battle of Visby in Gotland, 1361.
(A) This armour consists of 29 plates riveted to a support of leather or linen; it is of a type which appeared at the end of the 13th century in Continental Europe.
(B) This form with fewer and larger plates is regarded as a later style. (National Historical Museum, Stockholm)

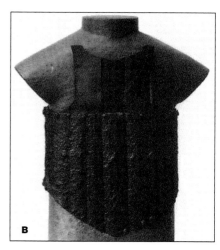

A

B

fewer flat surfaces, in an attempt to ensure that blows glanced off harmlessly. For horsemen the most noticeable new style was the bascinet, which could incorporate a moveable visor of either the 'pig-face' or 'dog-face' shape. In addition to providing very effective protection for head, neck and face, the bascinet also usually had a mail aventail attached to its rim to cover the neck and throat.

A distinctive form of bascinet found only in northern Europe and surviving in a single specimen from Poland is now known as the 'Order helmet', reflecting its supposed association with the military order of Teutonic Knights. The face was protected by a visor and the helmet had an aventail. The lower part was essentially the same as that of ordinary bascinets, but the upper part was extended into a tall point rather like the traditional helmets of Russia and further east; this helmet therefore seems to be a fusion of Western and Eastern styles.

Beneath these various forms of helmets it was still common to wear a mail coif with a padded cloth coif underneath. For footsoldiers the most visible development was a near universal adoption of various forms of brimmed kettle-hats or chapels-de-fer; this type had been developed during the 13th century but really came into its own during the following century. A special form of kettle-hat developed in Scandinavia had a rounder skull and a narrower brim.

It is worth noting that infantrymen seemed inclined to continue using helmets that did not cover their faces and hardly impaired their vision at all. The reasons are probably found in the different methods of combat employed by heavily armoured mounted troops and the generally more lightly equipped footsoldiers. Nevertheless, the chapel-de-fer was also used by mounted troops, although less frequently than among the infantry. Meanwhile, infantrymen gradually adopted pieces of armour previously developed for cavalry use, including more wrist- and knee-length mail habergeons, sometimes with mail mittens, and occasionally mail chausses for the legs. Even so, it still remained generally true that men on foot preferred to carry less armour than riders, because there was no horse to share their burden.

Shields generally became smaller and, for mounted combatants, emerged as what is today widely known as the 'heater-shaped shield'. Infantry continued to use larger shields although, towards the end of the 14th century, there was a tendency for foot soldiers to abandon shields altogether. Shields were, nevertheless, an area in which Scandinavian developments differed from most of Europe, since the buckler or small hand-held shield became increasingly popularity. It could take many shapes, the simplest being little more than a shield-boss with a small wooden shield around it. The diameter of such bucklers normally ranged from 12 to 16in (30–40cm) with a sturdy hand-grip behind or within the boss. The wooden surface of a buckler could also be strengthened with decoratively shaped metal reinforcements on the front surface while the rims were often strengthened by strips of leather to prevent splitting.

Wall or ceiling painting of St Olaf, with the axe which was the symbol of his martyrdom. The painting was made c.1380; the long-shafted axe now seems to have the socket extended into a hammer-like head on the back. It was almost a forerunner of the poleaxe, indicating that the long-hafted axe wielded with two hands continued to be in use throughout the Middle Ages. (*in situ* Skamstrup church, Denmark)

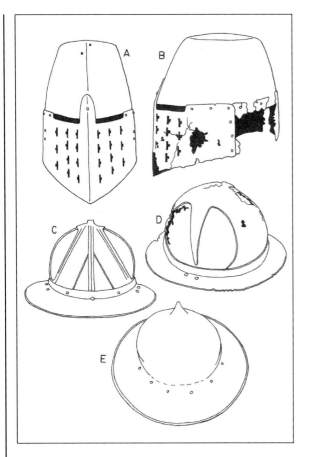

Helmets, from the end of the
13th to the mid 15th centuries:

(A) Reconstruction of the great
helm found in the castle of
Aranaes, c.1300

(B) The great helm found at
Aranaes, in its original condition
(National Historical Museum,
Stockholm)

(C) Norwegian 'kettle' helmet
or chapel-de-fer, 13th century
(National Historical Museum,
Stockholm)

(D) 'Kettle' helmet, 14th–15th
century (Museum of Estonian
History, Tallinn)

(E) Danish 'kettle' helmet, first
half of the 15th century (Royal
Danish Arsenal Museum,
Copenhagen)

## Weapons

Here the main developments were associated with missile weapons and infantry pole-arms.

It was during the 14th century that gunpowder reached Scandinavia and the Baltic, the Teutonic Knights and Danish armies being relatively earlier than Sweden and Norway in the use of this new technology. Early hand-held guns were little more than miniaturized cannons, and would have been more effective in frightening an enemy than in doing much physical harm. Such devices did, however, prove useful when attacking or defending fortifications, where the man with a gun could fire from behind considerably better cover than was possible with a bow or crossbow – the vertical and horizontal staves of the latter needed more space and they were shot through larger embrasures. On the other hand, firing mechanisms were so unreliable that guns could only be used effectively in static conflicts such as sieges.

During the 14th century the crossbow was developed further. Increases in its reliability and power reflected both improved techniques of manufacture and higher quality materials. The crossbow now seems to have replaced the hand-bow almost entirely. The bolts shot by such weapons remained essentially the same as before, their points being mostly of the basic armour-piercing bodkin shape, though such points now tended to be shorter and squatter than those on arrows to be shot from hand-bows.

The sword similarly underwent minor changes, but these were to a large extent cosmetic, changing the appearance of the weapon rather than the way in which it was used. A surviving weapon known as the Tritonia Sword is a good example of a type that was very popular as a horseman's weapon during the later 13th and first half of the 14th century. It is also necessary to point out that, while typologies of sword blades can shed light on the emergence of newer or more fashionable forms, the older or more traditional ones remained in production at the same time.

One innovation which appeared during the late 13th and early 14th centuries was the longsword. This was a development of the earlier horseman's single-handed war sword and was, in effect, an enlarged version with a longer blade which made it easier for a man on horseback to reach his target. This new form was then developed further into a separate class of weapon, for use both on horseback and on foot. In reality the type of sword used by an individual was almost certainly a matter of individual preference or was simply what a particular employer saw fit to issue to his followers.

This was the century during which the dagger became more prominent as a fighting weapon, at least in the sense that it was increasingly often depicted in pictorial sources. These show that daggers were specifically weapons rather than also serving more utilitarian functions. The 14th century fighting dagger relied on its point to inflict damage, allowing the weapon to be thrust into the most vulnerable chinks in the jointed areas of armour. Contrary to a widespread modern belief, the slashing type of attack using the edge of a dagger was quite useless even against an opponent wearing ordinary clothing, while a thrust could penetrate deep into the vital organs without much effort.

The mace remained in use, as did other forms of weapons which relied on weight. Amongst the other edged weapons would have been the axe, but this did not see any significant changes. It does seem that the earlier type of long-hafted axe wielded with two hands now fell into disuse, perhaps as a result of the development of more efficient pole-arms which combined an axe blade with other useful features. One of the most significant developments during the 14th century was this combining of thrusting and slashing blades into one weapon, of which the halberd would eventually become the most developed type. Its basic design was nevertheless simple: one or more cutting blades were added to a substantial spear shaft to create a hugely improved weapon. The precise date when these new cut-and-thrust weapons appeared is not known, but they were clearly present in Continental Europe in the first half of the 14th century and in Scandinavia during the second half of that century. Meanwhile the spear remained an important weapon, but would gradually be replaced by early forms of halberds amongst professional soldiers if not yet among local militias.

## ARMOUR & WEAPONS, 1400–1500

The major directions of technological change in 15th century Scandinavian military equipment were towards more plate armour, and an increased reliance on more complex forms of pole-arms. Another feature of this century was the fact that crusading efforts shifted away from the Scandinavian countries and were henceforth mostly limited to the Teutonic Knights and the German-speaking regions south of the Baltic.

During the 15th century armour tended to develop into more specialized forms. New techniques also meant that it was often quicker and cheaper to manufacture items of plate rather than of ringmail. Plate not only gave better protection but also permitted increased mobility, largely because the old fashioned, thickly padded soft armours worn beneath mail could now largely be dispensed with – the better fitting plate armour required little or no such padding. Furthermore, the armour became modular rather than covering large areas of the body with single pieces of iron or steel. This even included the torso, which could now be covered with two large pieces for the front and for the back, each of which often consisted of two separate elements, resulting in a better fit and greater mobility. Meanwhile mail declined in importance in favour

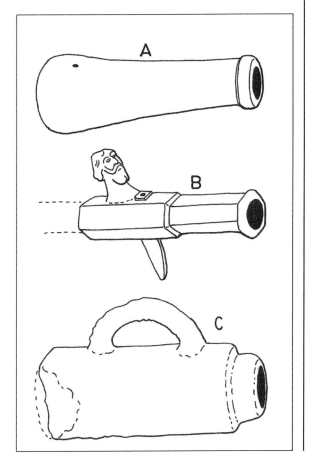

(A) Bronze gun-barrel from Loshult, Skåne, Sweden; length, 11.8in/30 cm; early 14th century. (National Historical Museum, Stockholm)

(B) Bronze barrel of a late 14th century hand-gun; length, 7.5in/19cm. (National Historical Museum, Stockholm)

(C) Removeable iron breech from a cannon, 15th century. Such weapons were probably supplied with multiple breeches; loaded separately and then fixed into the rear of the barrel by means of a wedge between the breech and part of the carriage, these allowed rapid fire. (Museum of Estonian History, Tallinn)

of plate armour, often only being included as a means of covering vulnerable gaps in plate defences at the armpits, elbows and groin.

Small plates could be attached to a flexible garment to form a scale-lined brigandine, which resulted in a relatively tight-fitting jacket, usually sleeveless. For mounted soldiers, pieces of plate armour now covered their legs, sometimes with mail underneath. The soldier's upper body was covered first with a thin arming jacket, on top of which went plate armour covering the torso, arms and shoulders. Although almost all styles of armour corresponded to a general model, there were significant regional variations and different solutions to specific problems. The jupon was a padded garment that developed out of the earlier gambeson but was tailored to follow the contours of the body, and was often worn on the outside of an armour. This enabled the jupon to double as a warm outer garment in cold weather.

The 'kettle-hat' retained essentially the same shape, but occasionally borrowed features from other popular helmets such as the sallet. This resulted in an interesting version which had a deeper and wider brim with a slit for the eyes. Wide brimmed chapels-de-fer were most common among footsoldiers, but sometimes fully armoured riders used them: they offered excellent protection plus improved visibility.

## Weapons

The 15th century was characterized by a continuation of several 14th century developments, most notably towards better pole-arms, stronger crossbows and more efficient use of gunpowder, the latter resulting in greater numbers of more powerful cannons and hand-held guns. However, the change in weapons technology that had the most direct impact on the way battles were fought was the fully developed halberd and poleaxe.

The former now consisted of a shaft about 50–80in (c.130–200mm) long, with a metal head which incorporated not only a cutting edge and thrusting point but often one or more sharpened hooks. The great advantage of this weapon was its remarkable ease of use, while also being highly effective against both heavily and lightly armoured foes. To achieve its best effect this halberd was intended to be used by men in formation. Other styles of pole-arm also developed, including new forms of spear such as those with additional horizontal cross-bars, as shown in Dolnstein's famous drawings. This remained in use into the Renaissance period, when it evolved into weapons such as the partisan and the pike.

The poleaxe was another characteristic development of the late 14th and early 15th centuries. It came to be regarded as a distinctively knightly or chivalrous weapon, and found particular favour in Continental Europe, though it was less popular in Sweden and Norway. Taken into widespread use in Germany, the poleaxe was consequently taken up by the Teutonic Knights and German crusaders, who introduced it to the Baltic region.

The major development in 15th century swords was a further evolution of the longsword, resulting in an almost perfect design which was now the preferred aristocratic weapon. Several such longswords have been found in noble tombs in the Swedish diocese of Lund. In battle the longsword had originally been the weapon of a mounted knight rather than a footsoldier, but now it seems to have required the use of both hands to be effective. Only the strongest armour could withstand the longsword, a particularly fine example being seen in a statue of St George slaying the Dragon in Storkyrkan, Stockholm, which commemorated the Swedish victory at the battle of Brunkeberg (see opposite).

During the 15th century the so-called ballock dagger became a near-universal male accessory, while the rondel dagger also developed into a fearsome close-combat weapon; its slender but very sturdy blade could be used against the most strongly armoured opponent. The importance of the dagger can also be seen in the 'Fight Books' of this period, where texts dealing with the sword and buckler are now few, while large shields are entirely absent; in contrast, sections dealing with the use of a sword and dagger were abundant.

Where crossbows were concerned, the bowstave became notably stronger while the manner of spanning the weapon changed in consequence, with the adoption of the crank, goat's-foot or windlass mechanisms.

# MILITARY EQUIPMENT IN THE BALTIC LANDS & NOVGOROD

The regions along the eastern side of the Baltic Sea experienced influences from the Eurasian steppes that were never felt in Scandinavia, although they did reach several parts of Central Europe. This had the effect that, while the basic types of military equipment used along the eastern and south-eastern shores of the Baltic differed very little from those of Scandinavia and Western Europe, their decorations and some aspects of their style or appearance could differ considerably.

Pagan Prussian statues, mostly in the form of armed warriors, perhaps used as gravemarkers or for some other religious purpose; they were found in what is now the Russian enclave of Kaliningrad, ex-Königsberg. The swords suggest that they date from the 10th to 12th centuries. Note that two of the rear views seem to show a round, slung shield, and a hood with a large liripipe. At centre, a cap with an upturned flap resembles that which we reconstruct in Plate F1. Most of these figures have drinking horns. (after V.I.Kulakov)

Estonian and Scandinavian
weapons, ranging from the 10th
to 12th centuries. (Museum
of Estonian History, Tallinn;
photograph D.Nicolle)

The major influence was, of course, from the great nomadic horse-based cultures of the steppes. This was present from at least the early 6th century onwards. Unfortunately, there are as yet fewer surviving examples of medieval military equipment from these regions than from Western Europe; but as archaeological research develops further, the historians of these countries will be able to delve more deeply into their military-technological history.

### 1100–1300

The mail shirt was the standard form of body armour along the southern and eastern shores of the Baltic, as it was in Scandinavia during this period. But there was also use of a form of scale armour, consisting of small metal scales sewn on to an undergarment of leather or several layers of cloth. Padded soft armours similar to the gambeson were also present.

Helmets basically corresponded to those found in Scandinavia, while there were distinctive local or eastern styles, including those in which the top narrowed into a point about 8in (20cm) high. It was also quite common to attach a mail aventail to the rim of a helmet to provide additional protection. Mail coifs were similarly used, although mail leggings do not seem to have become as popular as they were in Western Europe. Perhaps it was the influence of the great horse cultures of the East which precluded items that tended to impede horsemanship.

As elsewhere, the use of mittens and hand protections were important; again as in Western Europe, plate reinforcements were used. It is possible that this was an ongoing tradition from the earlier Viking Age, while at the same time being influenced by the Eurasian steppe cultures, especially as the use of bone or metal reinforcements might elsewhere have been regarded as an archaic technique by the medieval period. Similarly the pointed style of helmet that became common in this area can be traced back to a common root that was present from India to the Baltic. This form of helmet essentially consisted of a round base which narrowed acutely or more gently to a narrow top.

The shields used east and south-east of the Baltic coast were initially of the same round type as used in Scandinavia during the same period. These continued to be used, but were later supplemented with the kite-shaped and so-called 'heater' types of shield. The way in which these shields were constructed was probably much the same as elsewhere, though as yet there is not enough archaeological evidence to state this with certainty. A base of wooden boards would have been covered with one or more layers of leather, parchment or even, on occasions, with fur. The round shield would always have had a boss, and some form of reinforcement around the rim to prevent the boards splitting. The exterior of such shield could, of course, be painted in designs or colours.

## Weapons

The weapons were much the same as those used by other European peoples. Swords and axes remained the favourite edged weapons, and these could be wielded with one hand. There is little evidence for the use of long-hafted axes wielded with two hands such as those seen in Scandinavia. Most swords were of the double-edged, straight-bladed type, using very much the same language of form as seen further west. Weighty weapons such as the mace were popular, especially for use on horseback, as was also true of spears and lances.

The bow was a particularly important weapon in the Baltic regions, having long been used by the hunting communities of these sparsely populated lands. As such it doubled as a weapon of war and a tool for survival in a difficult climate. On the other hand, the crossbow does not seem to have achieved the same popularity as it did in Scandinavia or Continental Europe. Inevitably, these bows have left little trace in the archaeological record; yet there is no reason to suppose that they were different from those used on the other side of the Baltic. The size and weight of the bows might, however, have differed. Longbows are known to have been used in Europe from the early Bronze Age onwards, so their design was clearly known; on the other hand, a smaller bow is easier to use as a hunting weapon in dense forest.

ABOVE **Part of a 13th century wall-painting at Garda on the Swedish island of Gotland, which seems to have been painted by an artist from the East. The eastern influences are seen in the helmets of the horsemen, which still do not have the face-guards which were otherwise normal in Europe at this time. The shields are of the smaller 'heater' type; and note that the spears have crossbars, which is usually a feature of hunting weapons.** (*in situ* **Garda Church, Gotland, Sweden**)

LEFT **Another detail from the 13th century Garda wall-painting; these helmets are significant. The man on the right has a tall, pointed or 'spired' style of the type commonly seen in Russia or in Byzantine art. The man in the centre wears some form of brimmed 'kettle-hat'.** (*in situ* **Garda Church, Gotland, Sweden**)

It is an interesting possibility that Lithuanian and Russian forces may have had access to the Magyar form of bow, which was a composite weapon, widely used by the peoples of the steppes and eastern forests before the spread of the shorter but thicker Turco-Mongol bow. Not only were new waves of steppe peoples pushing into Eastern and Central Europe from the 12th century onwards, but Huns and others had been migrating into what is now Hungary and some surrounding regions from a much earlier date. All of these peoples relied to a great extent upon archery and used various forms of composite bow. Such bows would have been smaller in overall size than those of simple one-piece wooden construction commonly used in Europe. In Russia and some other parts of the far north of eastern Europe and western Asia, a form of bow made of more than one piece of wood and sometimes reinforced by bone or antler, was also widespread. In some respects its construction had elements in common with the fully composite bow of wood, sinew and horn, and may indeed have been its archaeological predecessor.

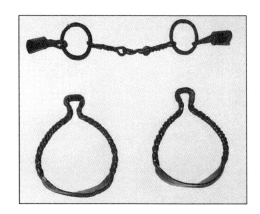

A horse's bit and a pair of bronze stirrups from a 12th century Estonian grave. These items are closer in style to those used by the nomadic peoples of the steppes in southern Russia than to Western European forms, and show that the area on the eastern shores of the Baltic Sea absorbed technological influences from the East as well as from the West. (Museum of Estonian History, Tallinn; photograph D.Nicolle)

Iron caltrops used as a defence against cavalry attack; Estonia, 13th–14th century. (Museum of Estonian History, Tallinn; photograph D.Nicolle)

The most common pole-arm was the spear, as it was in Scandinavia, and was of similar construction, although the spearheads were not very large in comparison to some earlier Viking Age spear blades. Most were around 7–8in (17–20cm) long and, when used for hunting such animals as boars, would have incorporated a crossbar. A knife of some sort would have been almost universally carried, in designs ranging from the early single-edged utility knife to the later forms of specialized fighting knives.

## 1300–1500

Armour in the Baltic region initially developed in much the same way as it did in Scandinavia and the rest of Europe. One major difference, however, seems to be that true plate armour did not achieve such wide popularity in the eastern Baltic countries, Novgorod and the rest of Russia as it did elsewhere in Europe. The reasons for this are unclear, but may include the absence of a 'chivalrous culture' with its associated tournaments and other such aristocratic activities, which encouraged the development of heavier armour within Europe. Another possibility is that plate armour simply did not serve any useful purpose in the sort of warfare that erupted between the resurgent native Finn and Balt populations and the crusading armies and military orders. The very nature of the densely forested countryside and the relative lack of large face-to-face battles on open ground would have rendered heavy armour almost useless.

*(continued on page 33)*

THE DANISH INVASION OF THE ISLAND OF
RÜGEN, 1168–1169
1: King Valdemar I of Denmark
2: Danish knight
3: Slav nobleman from
   Baltic coast

A

BUILDING OF A TIMBER FORT, LATE 12TH CENTURY
1: Danish knight
2: Danish sergeant
3: Captured Estonian warrior

B

DANISH CRUSADE AGAINST THE ESTONIANS, 1219
1: Danish knight
2: Low-status crusader
3: Danish sergeant

C

SWEDISH DEFEAT BY PRINCE ALEXANDER NEVSKI, 1240

1: Swedish knight
2: Swedish infantry sergeant
3: Swedish sailor or boatman

SWEDISH CRUSADERS, c.1275
1: Swedish knight
2: Swedish sergeant with spanned crossbow
3: Finn auxiliary with pack-mule

E

THE GATES OF DANISH REVAL, EARLY 14th CENTURY
1: Danish crossbowman
2: Lithuanian nobleman
3: Teutonic brother knight

F

KING MAGNUS OF SWEDEN INVADES RUSSIA, 1348
1: King Magnus Eriksson of Sweden
2: Swedish knight
3: German mercenary

SWEDISH ATTACK ON MUSCOVITE FORTRESS, 1496
1: Swedish artilleryman
2: Finnish crossbowman
3: Swedish man-at-arms

An 11th or 12th century spearhead from Finland, with curved extensions each side of the socket. (National Museum, Helsinki)

Of considerably greater importance was the increasing volume of equipment available to the ordinary footsoldiers who, as the years passed, acquired larger mail shirts, mail coifs and coats-of-plates, which offered good protection without hampering movement or being too heavy. It is important to understand that this was an example of an exchange of influences between Western Europe and the eastern regions of the Baltic and even further east. Similarly, there was a continued use of metal reinforcements to protect the arms, primarily in the form of 'splints' or strips of metal, 'elbow cups' and improved hand defences.

When these changes and developments are viewed as a whole, it seems that it was the invading crusading armies that had to adapt to local circumstances, rather than local peoples copying the invaders. On the other hand the use of padded armour of various designs became just as important for local fighting men as it was for the invading crusaders. Of course, such garments also offered insulation, and the continued use of leather and furs against the biting cold of the Baltic winter remained an important aspect of military equipment in this region.

# STRATEGY & TACTICS

The Northern or Baltic Crusades went through several phases, their strategy and tactics often being adapted to suit changing circumstances and challenges. In many ways these campaigns became a war of endurance on all sides; it was very difficult and costly, especially for Denmark and Sweden, to support their conquests on the far side of the Baltic Sea. Since neither had large armies, those forces which were sent soon found themselves greatly outnumbered by the local inhabitants. The struggle thus became one of establishing or removing a series of strongpoints. These proved to be the best, and perhaps the only means by which the Scandinavian crusaders could control conquered territory.

To face the indigenous Estonians and Latvians the Danish or Swedish crusading armies numbered no more than 4,000 troops. Such small numbers made the initial conquest of large areas very difficult; this was the main reason why the Baltic area saw the building of many more castles than was the case in Denmark and Sweden themselves. By constructing such a strongpoint the occupiers could gradually extend their control outwards through a policy of combined military action, co-operation, trade and politics, thus eventually taking over a larger territory. New fortifications could then be built further away, and the process repeated as often as necessary.

Crusading armies simply never had enough men to conquer the Baltic region outright – in fact, they often found themselves besieged within their castles, surrounded by a sea of enemies. Such a strategy and its associated tactics were to a large extent dictated by the fact that the area was almost completely covered by dense forests or lakes. This also had the effect of making rivers and other waterways extremely important avenues of movement for both sides. As a result, castles tended to be erected close for such vital lines of communication.

Scandinavian seals, illustrating types of Baltic shipping:
(Top) Seal of the city of Bergen, dating from 1376, showing that the older type of Scandinavian ships used in the early crusades were still in use – or at least still had symbolic resonance. The references to the old Viking longship are obvious.

(Below) Seal of the city of Stralsund, 1329 – half a century before that of Bremen – showing a *kogg*, with raised forecastle and sterncastle. This type of vessel, in various sizes, was the most common ship type in the Baltic for several centuries.

In Europe the warfare of the medieval period focused to a great extent on the taking or holding of castles and fortified towns. Such campaigns also laid considerable emphasis on sending relief to such places when they were cut off, threatened or under attack. If a place fell or surrendered, it normally accepted its new lords – who could, in their turn, subsequently expect to endure another siege as the previous proprietors attempted to reclaim that location. However, this mode of warfare was not the prevailing pattern in the Baltic Crusades, at least not after the initial invasions of the coastal areas. From the Iron Age onward settlements and towns had sprung up along these coasts as a result of trade. Some of these towns were already quite large, but were quickly besieged and conquered by the crusaders. The construction of strongpoints, usually in the form of castles, became a very important aspect of subsequent warfare, but besieging such places was neither the only nor even the major method of conducting warfare.

Instead, the Baltic Crusades were largely a matter of skirmishes and raids, during which occasional set-piece battles occurred – normally only when both sides believed that they could achieve tactical advantages in such a confrontation. Furthermore, the terrain did not allow for very imaginative manoeuvring; the movements of troops tended to be relatively predictable, and available routes were strictly limited by geography and vegetation. Rapid forays into enemy territory did play an important role, yet the groups of men involved would have been small, ranging from a couple of hundred to perhaps a thousand troops.

One severe limitation was that such raiding forces had to carry all their own provisions, inhibiting the time that they could be in the field. There was little opportunity for them to live off such generally unproductive land. Consequently, campaigning in this region was reminiscent of the chevauchée raids of the Hundred Years' War between England and France. The main goals of these raids were to disperse the enemy and destroy his resources, depopulating a region by obliterating crops and dwellings, and then retreating before the enemy could counter-attack. The local terrain tended to pose problems even in this form of warfare: the many lakes, rivers, streams, bogs and marshes formed such hazardous and sometimes unpredictable barriers that it was all too easy for the raiders to get caught by a rising lake or a ford that was no longer passable because of unexpectedly heavy rain or melting snow. Because the raiding parties were themselves relatively limited in number, they could not afford to get caught by defending forces against such natural obstacles. As a consequence, the Teutonic Knights, with their very limited numbers of men, made a point of dividing their raiding forces into small detachments, in order to minimize possible losses if a party got itself cut off or trapped.

Raiding was safest when it was carried out relatively close to friendly forts, and along the Rivers Dvina and Niemen. This was because, in a country that offered so few roads and so many obstacles, provisions were always a problem. Since each man had to carry whatever he needed, poor planning or unforeseen mishaps sometimes resulted in soldiers having to eat their own pack-animals – and even, on more than one occasion, their horses.

An example of the problems presented by the Baltic terrain is provided by a Swedish thrust towards the lake and town of Ladoga from the Swedish castle of Viborg in 1295. Troops were sent into the Ladoga region and erected a fort known as Keksholm; but its garrison was wiped out by a Novgorodian counter-attack the very same year. It simply proved impossible to maintain a castle around 200 miles' travelling distance from the nearest friendly strongpoint; that 200 miles had to be travelled by water, because the direct overland distance of just 50 miles was impassable. The problem of supporting forward outposts was much the same throughout the entire region, and as a result the odds were stacked heavily in favour of the defending population. In crude terms, the Novgorodian or Lithuanian forces, operating within their own territories, were capable of absorbing and then swamping the invading crusaders.

During the early years of the Baltic Crusades it was customary to slaughter all captives out of hand, with the exception of the peasants and labourers who were still required to cultivate the land for their new masters. On these wild frontiers captured fighting men were killed regardless of the status of the victim or his killer. This was not normal behaviour within Western Christendom, and as more crusaders arrived, particularly during the 14th century, there began to be more observance of the familiar practice of taking prisoners for ransom. This in turn resulted in parleys or brief truces to negotiate the release of captives. Naturally, since he normally had no means of raising a ransom, the ordinary footsoldier could still expect little mercy if he fell into enemy hands.

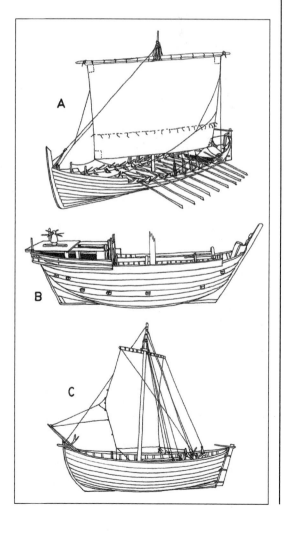

**Baltic shipping:**
**(A)** Boat 5 from Helgeandsholmen, dated to the first decade of the 14th century; this is an interesting example of a *snäcka* of a type used by the *ledung* armies during the preceding centuries. It had a length of 72ft/22m and a beam of 11.5ft/3.5m. An important change from the earlier Viking period is that the rudder is now fixed to the sternpost. The ship could be sailed as well as rowed, and would have been ideal for disembarking troops because of its ability to navigate shallow waters.

**(B)** Reconstruction of the hull of the Bremer *kogg*, dated to the 1380s; in addition to the missing mast and rigging, there would also have been a substantial superstructure at the stern.

**(C)** Reconstruction by Harald Åkerlund of a ship found at Kalmar and dating from the mid-13th century. This was a freight transport, with a length of 36ft/11m and a beam of 14.9ft/4.55 metres.

The castle of Åbo in south-western Finland. Originally constructed in the 1280s to support a Swedish crusade in this region, it was subsequently enlarged, most notably in the second half of the 14th century.

Viborg Castle in south-eastern Finland, dating from the late 14th century.

## Climate and terrain

The climate of the Baltic region is mild enough during summer, although spring and autumn often see very heavy rains. This, when coupled with severe winters and heavy snowfall, made warfare difficult at certain seasons of the year. For example, the records tell us that on one winter campaign the Teutonic Knights had to travel in single file because it was impossible to pass through the deep snow which lay on either side of their path; the tactical hazards of such a march formation in thick forest need no emphasis. The extreme cold that occasionally strikes the Baltic region could also be crippling, especially to animals, and the records again indicate that during hard winters horses could die in such large numbers that the cavalry were left without sufficient mounts.

Such a combination of difficult terrain, seasonal snow and spring and autumn rains made campaigning in these regions an extremely harsh challenge, and took a great toll of both men and equipment. Clearly, these climatic obstacles almost invariably worked in favour of the local or indigenous defenders, who were accustomed to these conditions and were operating in a climate with which they were familiar. Circumstances could become even more difficult for the crusaders if there was a mild, wet winter when the ground did not freeze; at such times the entire countryside seemed to turn into an impassable bog, haunted by clouds of biting insects after the arrival of warmer weather.

The result of all these factors was that a sort of no-man's-land soon emerged between the fighting parties. This could consist of stretches of rough terrain up to perhaps 120 miles (190km) wide, with no real roads and in which only the waterways offered passable routes.

## Winter warfare

The idea of fighting during winter was not normally regarded as sensible in Continental Europe, but in Scandinavia it was traditionally seen as a suitable season for any army that could cope with the cold. In a region where even well-established dirt roads were simply non-existent across wide swathes of the country, it was actually easier to campaign in cold winters than in summer, because the waterways were normally frozen and thus provided easy routes for travel by sleigh and on horseback. Even the forests tended to be easier to penetrate, because sleighs could operate in anything except the softest and deepest snow. The only practical alternative was to make at least part of the journey by coastal shipping.

The use of skis and sleighs was well documented throughout the entire Scandinavian and Baltic region. Although not suitable for transporting large number of troops, skis did permit easy scouting in wintertime. The use of horse-drawn sleighs provided a practical method of transporting equipment and supplies during a campaign – indeed, the only method that could be adopted during crusading expeditions other than using the rivers. Winter warfare thus became more or less a necessity rather than a matter of choice; in the milder seasons it was often impossible to transport heavy loads deep inland or to any distance away from the main waterways. Conversely, however, winter campaigning required substantially larger supplies of food and even of equipment in order to maintain a crusading force at an effective level of fitness and fighting capability.

Sleighs were pulled by horses harnessed singly or in pairs, which could easily pull many hundreds of pounds weight if packed on a well-made sleigh. Troops were normally obliged to march on foot if they had no horses to ride. Riding horses themselves were generally not well suited to winter campaigning. During one especially bitter winter the Teutonic Knights lost an estimated one thousand horses, which represented virtually their entire stock and thus reduced them to an infantry force until replacement mounts could be obtained. Once the initial conquest of the coastal regions had been completed and the area of control had been pushed up the major waterways, the campaigns had to be extended into the wintertime if further progress was to be made. Normally there were two forays during each winter, one in December and one in January or February, with some time between these expeditions for the Christmas celebrations. The crusaders were able to pursue this twin campaigning strategy partly as a result of the fact that a number of their main bases were located on the coasts, which made it easier for them to ship in supplies throughout much of the year. By contrast the Lithuanians, who lived inland, found it much more difficult to procure supplies during winter.

The city walls and outer towers of Tallinn (Reval), as they appeared in the late 19th century before the city spread much beyond its medieval fortifications.

## Boats and ships

Seafaring capability and a capacity to wage war on water was an important aspect of these conflicts, especially where Denmark and Sweden were concerned. For the Teutonic Knights and the other German crusaders this was also important but generally less so, as these southern participants had greater access to land communications.

The Scandinavian countries, most notably Norway and Denmark, continued to use later modifications of the old Viking Age longships right into the 14th century. This style of ship, known as a *snäcka* in Sweden, was an ideal vessel for transporting troops, being able to carry around 25 men plus their equipment, and being extremely seaworthy. It was equipped with oars, which made it less susceptible to being becalmed, and which also enabled such vessels to navigate estuaries, rivers and lakes. This versatility, along with its shallow draught, made the *snäcka* suitable for both transporting and putting ashore men and equipment during various crusading campaigns.

The major disadvantage of the *snäcka* was that it was not particularly suitable for fighting on water when compared to the later *kogg*, which could carry more troops and was built in several different sizes. Being considerably higher in the water it proved to be a better fighting ship, especially when fitted with small fighting platforms or 'castles' for archers or crossbowmen fore and aft. The higher hulls of these vessels made it possible to shoot down on any enemy who was in a more old fashioned Viking-style ship.

The peoples who lived along the eastern and southern Baltic coasts were enthusiastic raiders, as the Scandinavians themselves had been in earlier years. Their ships are believed to have been very similar to the older Viking Age longships. This technological inferiority, plus the fact that crusader expeditions quickly seized control over most of the coasts, made actual sea battles virtually non-existent. Once the Christian mariners of the Baltic Sea abandoned longships in favour of *koggs*, any attempt by undecked, shallow-draught Baltic ships to tackle an armed Western vessel would almost certainly fail. Once the crusaders ventured far inland up the rivers, however, the balance might be more equal. The Lithuanians and Novgorodian Russians maintained fleets of river boats for the specific purpose of blocking vital waterways and avenues of communication.

## Fortifications

Castles are remarkably abundant in the Baltic region. Most were built by crusader sovereigns to guard their new holdings, by the military orders or by the bishops who also wielded significant military power in these lands. Meanwhile the native populations had their own traditions of fortification. As a result the Baltic Crusades were characterized by a style of warfare in which fortifications played an exceptionally important role – as was also the case in the Latin-Crusader

Castle plans:
(A) Gurre, Denmark

(B) Lihula, Estonia: 1 = citadel, 2 = first bailey, 3 = living quarters, 4 = stables, 5 = fosse, 6 = outer wall, 7 = quarry or pit, 8 = inner gate, 9 = entrance way, 10 = second bailey, 11 = moat, 12 = embankment, 13 = well and spring.

(C) Raseborg, Finland: 1 = line of old moat, 2 = line of new moat, 3 = natural water obstacle.

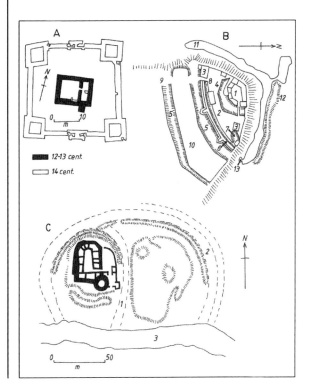

Middle East, where territory could not be held in the face of powerful invading forces without the presence of castles.

The earliest forms consisted of earthworks with timber additions, in the old Western European motte-and-bailey style; but these remained vulnerable to fire even in such technologically primitive warfare as that conducted by the peoples of the Baltic coastlands. The crusaders soon experienced this threat, and efforts were rapidly put in hand to build virtually fire-proof stone fortifications. Since the troops of Lithuania and even Novgorod had very little experience in siege warfare, such strongpoints gave the crusaders solid anchors for their areas of control. Over time more elaborate and occasionally quite large fortifications were constructed, the biggest probably being the Marienburg of the Teutonic Knights and the Viborg of the Swedes.

The earlier defensive works constructed by the local indigenous populations were mostly in naturally strong locations such as hilltops, bluffs or peninsulas, and they made full use of such terrain.

The so-called Virgin Tower which formed part of the inner defences between the Toompea Citadel and the medieval city of Reval. (D.Nicolle photograph)

When the crusaders conquered these regions they often rebuilt in the identical locations for the same tactical or strategic reasons. The remains of most fortifications in the Baltic lack an identifiable moat, since many of the locations were strong enough without this feature, their natural advantages sufficing to slow down an advancing enemy. This was particularly apparent when the castle was on top of a steep slope.

The quality of the actual fortification work tended to be high, especially those built by or for the Teutonic Knights. One reason may have been an exchange of personnel with the Order's holdings in the Middle East and other places where the science of military architecture was more advanced. Nevertheless, the sizes of the Baltic fortifications were general smaller than the epic fortresses in the crusader states of the eastern Mediterranean. Seeking to control a wide region, with a strictly limited number of troops but against an enemy lacking any sophisticated tradition of siege warfare, it was better for the crusader occupiers of the Baltic states to have numerous smaller, dispersed castles than a few very large regional centres.

## Siege warfare

Nevertheless, in unpacified country some kind of siege of one or more of their strongpoints was a constant possibility. As already pointed out, the one local resource in almost unlimited supply was timber – that is, solid fuel. Consequently it was normally only temporary strongpoints that were built of such materials once stone fortifications were being built.

Siege equipment in the form of mangonels, ballistas and other large missile-throwing or shooting devices were used by the crusaders when breaching the gates of local fortifications. Battering rams seem have been of the simple and relatively small hand-held type wielded by teams of men, but they proved effective enough. However, the most effective tactic when dealing with Baltic fortifications was simply to surround the place and starve its defenders into submission. Meanwhile efforts might also be made to torch it by approaching under the cover of fascines and stacking both wet and dry wood against the gate and timber palisade. The impact of smoke has often been overlooked by military historians when discussing the effectiveness of fire; dense smoke could effectively blind and choke the defenders and, under the right circumstances, might even lead to injury.

In their struggle against the invading crusaders the native populations used the simplest of siege devices such as ladders and ramps, but also sometimes stone-throwing machines. There seems to be no evidence for the use of sappers to undermine fortifications in these regions. Since they enjoyed a numerical advantage, it was often more economical in lives for local forces to blockade a crusader stronghold until its defenders either ran out of food or their morale collapsed. Any sortie by the small garrison usually failed for sheer lack of numbers. There were, however, several occasions when the besiegers needed to overcome the defenders as quickly as possible so as to avoid becoming trapped between a garrison and a relieving army. Even in such cases the small size of the garrison usually meant that an assault made under the cover of plentiful bows and crossbows was likely to succeed without incurring excessively heavy losses.

# AFTERMATH OF THE CRUSADES

The longer term results of the Baltic Crusades against the indigenous peoples of the region can be judged in a number of ways, and some of these developments had long-lasting ramifications.

In general terms, the conflicts in the Baltic seem to have spurred on the emergence there of more clearly defined linguistic and cultural regions, and thus eventually of nation states. It is almost certain that the gradual change from loose tribal confederations into more centralized forms of government reflected the need for more cohesive military forces with which the face the invading crusaders.

The defence or advance of Christianity against paganism had been the cornerstone of the Baltic crusading movement, and the vast state of Lithuania – the last pagan state in Europe – officially became Christian in 1386.

Within Scandinavia itself, the three nations of Denmark, Norway and Sweden were united from 1397 in the

The city walls of Tallin, the largest city and capital of Estonia. They mostly date from the late 14th century. There is a dramatic difference between the crowded interior of the old city on the left, as seen from the Paks Margareta or 'Fat Margaret' Tower towards the Great Coastal Gate, and the exterior of the medieval city which now consists of a public park. (D. Nicolle photograph).

troublesome Union of Kalmar, which had originally been suggested by Queen Margareta I. One significant effect of this union was a decline in Scandinavian interest in Baltic crusading. This more or less left the Teutonic Order on its own; the Order became an important power in Scandinavian regional politics during the tumultuous 15th century, but this development contributed to that Order's seemingly sudden collapse.

It is important to recognize that the Baltic region comprised a large number of diverse powers, but that all were linked by a common interest in trade. The Baltic Crusades were not, in any simple sense, directed against a common 'eastern enemy', but resulted in a shifting pattern of allegiances and alliances in which the

The keep of the castle of Raseborg, extensively restored in the late 19th century.

leaders of the Crusades always had to work pragmatically within the existing pattern of economic ties and interests. The raw materials and products extracted from the great northern forests and seas were of continuing value for many centuries; the importance of the salted fish, furs, walrus ivory and resins that Scandinavian seamen, hunters and trappers supplied to merchants from more southerly countries would soon be joined, and later overshadowed by the timber products that fed the great age of shipbuilding and world-wide navigation that was already dawning at the turn of the 15th and 16th centuries. Maintaining the delicate balance that regulated Baltic trade would become so increasingly important to other European nations that in time the major powers would be led to intervene directly in the region on several occasions.

At what we would today term the geopolitical level, the Baltic Crusades resulted in a number of very obvious developments. Sweden gained control of Finland, which was eventually drawn into the heart of the Swedish state rather than being merely a distant province. Finland would in fact play a very important strategic role, as well as being a significant source of manpower for Sweden, right up to the time when it was lost to Russia in 1808. Sweden also gained other provinces in the Baltic region, constructing several strong castles that would play an important part in the later Great Nordic War and in the Swedish expansions of the 17th and 18th centuries.

South of the Baltic, the kingdom of Poland emerged as a significant power on the eastern frontier of the German Empire, and would subsequently become an important participant in later European politics – linked for many years with Lithuania. Further east, Muscovy (Moscow) absorbed Novgorod and likewise grew into a major power, whose often warlike rivalry with Sweden lasted long after the end of the medieval period. In reality, the enmity between Russia and Sweden, which lasted from 1250 until 1808, was a consequence of the crusading movement, which led to a clash of their trading interests. It might be argued that the various struggles that swirled around the Baltic Crusades actually encouraged the unification of Novgorod and Moscow, leading to the development of the later Russian Tsarist state.

Meanwhile another and much more significant threat to Christendom was emerging far to the south-east, with the rise of the Ottoman Turks. This threat became acute during the late 15th and early 16th centuries, and consequently the old conflict between Orthodox Christian and Catholic Christian lands in eastern Europe and the Baltic became secondary. Europe's resources and efforts would now have to be invested on this new south-eastern frontier.

# FURTHER READING

Andersson, I., *A History of Sweden* (London, 1955)

Antiens, A., 'Structure and Manufacturing Techniques of Pattern-Welded Objects found in the Baltic States', *Journal of the Iron and Steel Institute* (1968) 563–571

Antiens, A., 'The Old Arms of Basilsimsa (History of the Ventspilskaya Okrug)', *Sovietskay Venta*, 50 (1983)

Benninghoven, F., *Der Orden der Schwertbrüder* (Cologne, 1965)

Bogdan, H., *Les Chevaliers Teutoniques* (Paris, 1995)

Bosi, R., *The Lapps: Ancient Peoples and Places Series* (London, 1960)

Bruiningh, H. Baron, 'Der älteste mittelalterliche Grabstein Livlands aus der St Martinkirche auf Holme bei Riga', in (anon. ed.), *Baltische Studien zur Archäologie und Geschichte, Arbeiten des Baltischen Vorbereitended Kometees für den XVI Archäologischen Kongress in Pleskau 1914* (Riga, 1914) 171–175

Brundage, J.A. (tr.), *The Chronicle of Henry of Livonia* (Madison, 1961)

Brundage, J.A., 'The Thirteenth-Century Livonian Crusades', *Jahrbücher für Geschichte Osteuropas*, n.s. XX (1972) 109

Christensen, A.E., 'Denmark between the Viking Age and the time of the Valdemars', *Mediaeval Scandinavia*, I (1966) 33–48

Christiansen, E., *The Northern Crusades: The Baltic and Catholic Frontier 1100–1525* (London, 1980)

Deveike, J., 'The Lithuanian Diarchies', *The Slavonic and East European Review*, XXVIII (1949–50) 392–397

Gimbutas, M., *The Balts: Ancient Peoples and Places Series* (London,1963)

Hajdu, P. (tr. G.F. Cushing), *Finno-Ugrian Languages and Peoples* (London, 1975)

Jutikkala, E., *A History of Finland* (London, 1962)

Kivikoski, E., *Die Eisenzeit Finlands* (Berlin, 1947)

Kivikoski, E., *Finland: Ancient Peoples and Places Series* (London, 1967)

Kulakov, V.I., *Istoriya Prussii do 1283 goda* (Moscow, 2003)

Larsson, L., *Kalmar unionens tid* (Stockholm, 1997)

Leppäaho, J., *Späteisenzeitliche Waffen aus Finnland: Schwertinschriften und Waffenverzierungen des 9.–12.Jahrnunderts* (Helsinki, 1964)

Lind, J., 'The Russian Sources of King Magnus Eriksson's campaign against Novgorod 1348–1351 – reconsidered', *Mediaeval Scandinavia*, XII (1988) 248–272

Lind, J., 'The Russian-Swedish Border according to the Peace Treaty of Nöteborg (Orekhovets-Pähkinälinna) and the Political Status of the Northern Part of Fennoscandia', *Mediaeval Scandinavia*, XIII (2000) 100–117

Lindholm, D., & D.Nicolle, *Medieval Scandinavian Armies (1) 1100–1300*,

Men-at-Arms No.396 (Oxford, 2003)

Lindholm, D., & D.Nicolle, *Medieval Scandinavian Armies (2) 1300–1500,* Men-at-Arms No.399 (Oxford, 2003)

Murray, V.(ed.), *Crusade and Conversion on the Baltic Frontier, 1150–1500* (Aldershot, 2001)

Musset, L., 'Problèmes militaries du Monde Scandinave (VII–XIIe siècle)', in *Settimane di Studi del Centro Italiano di Studi sull'Alto Medioevo* (Spoleto, 1968) 229–291

Musset, L., *Les Peuples Scandinaves au Moyen Age* (Paris, 1951)

Nicolle, D., *Armies of Medieval Russia 750–1250,* Men-at-Arms No.333 (Oxford, 1998)

Nicolle, D., *Lake Peipus 1242,* Campaigns No.46 (London, 1996)

Riley-Smith, J.(ed.), *Atlas of the Crusades* (London, 1991)

Sawyer, P. & B., *Medieval Scandinavia: From Conversion to Reformation circa 800–1500* (Minneapolis, 1993)

Sedov, V.V., *Finno-Ugrui i Baltui v Epokhu Srednevekovya* (Moscow, 1987)

Shpakovsky, V., & D.Nicolle, *Medieval Russian Armies 1250–1500,* Men-at-Arms No.367 (Oxford, 2002)

Skyum-Nielsen, N., & N.Lund (eds.), *Danish Medieval History: New Currents* (Copenhagen, 1981)

Slaski, K., 'Die dänisch-polnischen Beziehungen von dem Tode Valdemars II. bis zum Entstehen der Kalmarer Union', *Mediaeval Scandinavia,* IV (1971) 80–90

Smith, J.C., & W.Urban (tr.), *The Livonian Rhymed Chronicle* (Bloomington, 1977)

Urban, W., 'The Organisation and Defence of the Livonian Frontier in the Thirteenth Century', *Speculum,* XLVIII (1973) 523–532.

Urban, W., *The Baltic Crusade* (Chicago, 1994)

Urban, W., *The Prussian Crusade* (New York, 1980)

Urban, W., *The Samogitian Crusade* (Chicago, 1989)

Urban, W., *The Teutonic Knights: A Military History* (London, 2003).

Uustalu, E., *The History of the Estonian People* (London, 1952).

*Albert Collins armour can be seen and orders placed via his website:* www.viaarmorari.com

# PLATE COMMENTARIES

## A: THE DANISH INVASION OF THE ISLAND OF RÜGEN, 1168–1169

### A1: King Valdemar I of Denmark

Although Denmark was in close economic and cultural contact with neighbouring northern Germany, its military equipment was, like that of the other Scandinavian states, still rather old-fashioned. Therefore we have reconstructed the king here with good quality arms and armour, although it would have been seen as half a generation behind the times by a French or even an English observer. King Valdemar wears a one-piece iron helmet with integral nasal, over a mail coif with its ventail pulled across his throat and chin. His mail hauberk with its long sleeves and mittens is, however, of the latest design; it is worn over a quilted gambeson which probably replaced the more archaic felt 'soft armour'. His mail chausses are of the type which cover only the fronts and sides of his thighs, knees and legs, and are worn with soft leather boots. His shield, sword and sword belt are of designs which could have been seen in the late 11th century, but the decorations on his horse's harness follow the latest trends in Germany and northern France.

### A2: Danish knight

The seemingly archaic character of some Scandinavian armour is seen on this man, whose simple iron helmet has iron ear- and neck-pieces attached by short leather straps. His mail hauberk has an integral coif with a ventail across his mouth, but the sleeves are only of three-quarter length; the hauberk is slit at the sides, which was more for fighting on foot than on horseback. The scabbard is tied to the soft leather sword belt in the normal manner. The shield is of the long kite-shaped variety needed when the only other body protection was the mail hauberk; note his lack of leg protection. A knobbed bronze mace was typical of many parts of Scandinavia and the Baltic region.

## A3: Slav nobleman from Baltic coast

The Slav-speaking and as yet still pagan tribes of what is today north and north-eastern Germany were quite rich and had wide trading contacts, as well as the booty from their raiding; hence, this nobleman's military gear is relatively abundant and decorated. The iron helmet is probably of Polish or Russian origin, built up from four segments each with a raised reinforcing corrugation, riveted beneath an iron frame; but note that his simple mail hauberk lacks a coif. The neck of his linen shirt is closed by a gilded bronze brooch. He is armed with an abundantly decorated war-axe, plus a simple knife. The large round shield would be held on his fist rather than on his lower arm and hand, as was the case with most Western European shields. Here, as his village and idols burn, the ill-fated warrior was trying to save a horn sacred to the pagan god Svantevit.

## B: BUILDING OF A TIMBER FORT, LATE 12th CENTURY

### B1: Danish knight

By the late 12th century the Danish, and to a lesser extent the other Scandinavian kingdoms, had been drawn more closely into the mainstream of Western European culture. This was clearly reflected in the arms and armour of their military aristocracies. This knight has a high-domed, one-piece iron helmet of a type popular in Germany to the south. The ventail of the coif of his long-sleeved mail hauberk is here shown unlaced; one slightly old-fashioned note is struck by his mittens, which lack fingers and are more like extensions of the sleeves, whereas the very long skirts of his tunic again reflect German fashions. Beneath the mail hauberk and the tunic is a thickly quilted gambeson, and his legs are protected by mail chausses worn over normal woollen hose.

### B2: Danish sergeant

The increasingly popular flat-topped form of helmet was apparently also reflected in some helmets which were of two-piece construction. This lower-status sergeant's mail coif is here taken off his head, exposing its quilted lining. Again the man has a quilted form of soft armour beneath his mail hauberk, visible at his neck and below the hem of the hauberk. The bagginess of his leggings might indicate that they are trousers rather than more typically Western European hose; trousers continued to be worn in Scandinavia, particularly by

men of poorer origins. The blade of his spear has short curved lugs or 'wings', which were another archaic style, suitable for fighting on foot rather than on horseback.

### B3: Captured Estonian warrior

He appears to be a peasant warrior rather than a member of the indigenous Estonian aristocracy, his weapons being a substantial axe that might also have been a working tool, and a knife in a decorated leather sheath. The blade of the spear is a form found throughout the Baltic region, but the bronze standard was actually found in a Lithuanian or Prussian rather than an Estonian tribal area.

## C: DANISH CRUSADE AGAINST THE ESTONIANS, 1219

According to legend, it was during this campaign that the Danish flag fell miraculously from the sky at the battle of Lyndanise.

### C1: Danish knight

One again the arms, armour and even the clothing styles of this member of the Danish knightly aristocracy indicate strong German influence. The tall, two-piece iron helmet has a fixed iron visor, and is worn over a mail coif which forms an integral part of the mail hauberk. The visibly raised outline of a very thickly quilted gambeson worn beneath the hauberk and the surcoat can be seen at his shoulders. His legs and feet are now protected by complete, all-round mail chausses, though these have leather soles beneath his feet. The scabbard is still tied to the sword belt in a traditional manner; the knight is also armed with a massive bronze-headed mace, thrust beneath his saddle.

### C2: Low-status crusader

The directly riveted construction of this man's helmet might reflect Eastern rather than Western European influence, and would probably have been considered old-fashioned even in Scandinavia. His limited form of mail hauberk, baggy trousers, fighting knife and simple short-hafted infantry spear also show him to be a peasant or low-status warrior. The reality behind the story of how what became the Danish national flag 'fell from heaven' during this battle is, of course, unknown. Perhaps a blood-stained cloth might have been blown across the field of combat, being seen by some religiously excited crusaders as a white cross on a red background?

### C3: Danish sergeant

As a professional soldier, although one of humble origins, this Danish sergeant wears an early form of brimmed iron 'kettle-hat' – a style of helmet which became very popular throughout later medieval Scandinavia. Since he is fighting with a large axe wielded with both hands, he has slung his large kite-shaped shield on his back, held by its broad leather guige strap. The mail coif of his mail hauberk is again old-fashioned, lacking a ventail to be drawn across his chin and throat, but the hauberk itself is worn over a quilted soft-armour. The distinctive bronze hilt of his sword is often associated with Finland, and the weapon might be war-booty.

The seal of Birger Brosa, Sweden, late 12th century. The helmet and armour are typical for the time, although the face-guard – which was becoming increasingly common – is lacking here, and the helmet still has an old-fashioned nasal bar. The sword also looks more like a Viking Age weapon, with a broad groove and stubby quillons. See Plate A1. (Riksarkivet, Stockholm)

Swedish panel paintings, 13th century:
(Top left) Note at right the warrior with a flat-topped great helm, a shortened kite shield with a rounded top, and a surcoat.
(Top right) Both warriors wear full mail and carry swords, one having a smaller 'heater'-shaped shield slung on his back.
(Right) At left, two fully armoured knights on horseback, one with a great helm and the other with only a mail coif. (*in situ* Dädsjö Church, Småland, Sweden)

## D: SWEDISH DEFEAT BY PRINCE ALEXANDER NEVSKI, 1240

Defeated on the River Neva by the Prince of Novgorod in July 1240 during the Baltic First Crusade, these unfortunates try to escape by boat.

### D1: Swedish knight, mid-13th century

With his flat-topped great helm, full mail armour and partially padded surcoat, this knight looked essentially the same as fighting men of comparable status elsewhere in Western Europe. Only the fact that he wears boots over his mail chausses might indicate a local Scandinavian style, perhaps reflecting the weather in this part of Europe; his battleaxe, while unusual elsewhere in Western Europe, would not be entirely unknown. The shorter shield is a new fashion, as – apparently – are the quilted cuisses around his thighs and knees. The same applies to his horse's caparison, saddle and harness.

### D2: Swedish infantry sergeant

Most of this man's military equipment is again in the mid-13th century Western European mainstream. It consists of a low-domed one-piece iron helmet with an integral nasal; a full mail hauberk with a mail coif, here worn underneath a quilted cloth-covered coif; a full-length, long-sleeved quilted gambeson; and a modern style of short but broad – almost triangular – shield. On the other hand, the substantial fighting knife slung almost horizontally from his sword belt, and the baggy trousers worn over his close-fitting hose, are very Scandinavian or Baltic.

### D3: Swedish sailor or boatman

The one-piece, broad-brimmed iron 'war-hat' had by now become very widespread in Scandinavia. It was once again common for men from many backgrounds to carry a substantial knife or dagger. Otherwise this man's multiple layers of clothing, especially the broad-shouldered cape with a hood – here shown pushed back off the head – seem designed for working in a potentially cold and wet environment such as the Baltic Sea.

## E: SWEDISH CRUSADERS, c.1275

### E1: Swedish knight

The nature of warfare in and around the dense forests, bogs and lakes of Finland meant that some of the heaviest armour used in other parts of Europe was often unsuitable. This was usually a conflict of raid and ambush, in terrain without roads or very many passable tracks. This Swedish knight wears a

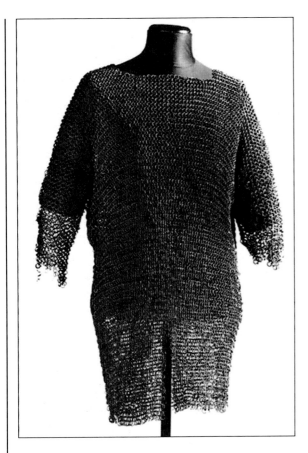

Mail habergeon or small form of hauberk, early 14th century; this piece is in fact English, but is entirely typical of armour of that period. The style would have been more or less the same since the late Viking Age, with only a lengthening of the arms and skirts to accommodate riders. (London Museum)

brimmed 'kettle-hat' or chapel-de-fer which does not interfere with his vision; its substantial cheekpieces are a distinctively Scandinavian feature. Otherwise, he has a German-style coat-of-plates beneath a separate mail coif and over a full mail hauberk, plus mail chausses for his legs.

### E2: Swedish sergeant with spanned crossbow
Walking with a spanned and loaded crossbow could be a dangerous thing to do, unless there was good reason to expect an ambush. The helmet worn by this sergeant may be old-fashioned in its basic shape, but is quite advanced in its corrugated or fluted reinforced surface. He otherwise relies on mail for protection, and is armed with a relatively short infantry-man's sword and a thick circular, wooden, buckler form of shield. In addition to a crossbow with a composite stave a crossbowman needed an iron spanning-hook on a belt around his hips, and a quiver to hold the short bolts or arrows.

### E3: Finn auxiliary with pack-mule
Local indigenous auxiliaries are known to have been less well armed than their Scandinavian rulers and colonizers. This man only has a rather ancient two-piece iron-framed helmet, though his sword is a fine old-fashioned weapon. His thick fur-lined coat would also have provided some protection.

## F: THE GATES OF DANISH REVAL, EARLY 14th CENTURY
### F1: Danish crossbowman
Northern Estonia and its main city of Reval (today called Tallinn) was all that remained of Denmark's crusading expansion by the 14th century, and would soon be sold to the Order of Teutonic Knights. Nevertheless, it was a valuable possession that would have been well guarded. Because of the biting north wind this crossbowman wears a fur-lined hat rather than a helmet; beneath this is a mail coif which also covers his shoulders. The outline of a thickly padded mail tippet or collar is also visible. Over his long-sleeved hauberk – which lacks mittens, because of his role as a crossbowman – he has a scale-lined coat-of-plates. His other equipment consists of a spanning-belt for his crossbow, a quiver for his bolts, a small wooden buckler, and a sword which has both a very old-fashioned pommel and much more modern down-curved quillons.

### F2: Lithuanian nobleman
Whether a fully armed Lithuanian nobleman would ever have approached the gates of Reval is unknown; however, this well-armed warrior represents the best equipped military elite of Europe's last pagan state. His helmet is of segmented construction with an iron frame; rawhide thongs threaded around the rim secure an internal lining, while the neckpiece is loosely riveted so that it can move slightly. He wears a gold torque around his neck and a gold armband above his elbow, below a short-sleeved mail hauberk. In addition to a short sword with a plain iron pommel and quillons whose scabbard hangs from a richly decorated belt, he is armed with a decorated spear and javelins. His prick-spurs are of a distinctive form, and are kept in place with leather straps and iron buckles.

### F3: Teutonic brother knight
The military orders usually had the best and most up-to-date equipment. Certainly this brother knight of the Teutonic Order is well armoured, with an early form of bascinet which has a hinged visor and a mail aventail attached to the inside of its rim; the broad, shoulder-covering part of this aventail also extends over part of the man's upper arms. The coat-of-plates opens only on the right shoulder, where an iron pin is threaded through iron staples. Beneath the coat-of-plates is a mail hauberk with three-quarter sleeves; additional arm protections are in the form of hardened leather rerebraces for the upper arms, splinted vambraces for the lower arms, and partially plated gauntlets. His chausses appear to be scale-lined, rather than with the usual ringmail. His massive single-edged falchion would be held in a scabbard that was slit down almost the full length of one side.

## G: KING MAGNUS OF SWEDEN INVADES RUSSIA, 1348
### G1: King Magnus Eriksson of Sweden
By the mid-14th century the military equipment of the ruling elite of Sweden and the other Scandinavian kingdoms was fully within the Western European – more particularly, German – tradition. Consequently King Magnus is shown with a deep form of bascinet with a face-covering mail flap, here in its lowered position, and a coat-of-plates beneath a heraldic surcoat. Under these he wears a mail hauberk, padded aketon or gambeson, rerebraces, vambraces and gauntlets; his leg armour is

similarly complete. He is armed with a knightly sword, a flanged mace, a substantial dagger, and a second saddle-sword beneath the flap of his saddle. In contrast, his horse harness is quite simple; note that much of the length of the reins is now made of chain rather than leather as a precaution against its getting severed in combat.

**G2: Swedish knight**
In contrast to the armour worn by his king, this ordinary Swedish knight wears old-fashioned gear, most notably his massive flat-topped great helm. It is worn over a separate mail coif which protects the neck but not the shoulders. Beneath this is the sleeveless surcoat and long-sleeved mail hauberk. His plated gauntlets are more up-to-date, but his leg armour is again very traditional. In contrast his swordbelt, sword, dagger and dagger-sheath suspension system are in a more recent style. He carries the Swedish battle standard known as the Folkunga Vapnet.

**G3: German mercenary**
Judging by his arms and armour, this mercenary commander passing on the report of his scouts comes from southern rather than northern Germany. Some degree of Italian stylistic and technological influence is visible, most obviously in his deep-brimmed steel 'war-hat' helmet. In other respects his body armour is similar to that of King Magnus, but includes guard-chains attached to the coat-of-plates beneath his surcoat; these will prevent the man losing his weapons in the tumult of battle. His haubergeon has broad three-quarter-length sleeves, which hang in pointed rear extensions behind his elbows. Under the fabric outer coverings his upper-arm rerebraces are lined with riveted iron splints, his gauntlets and thigh-covering cuisses with scales. The fact that the scales are on the exterior of his feet-protecting sabatons is probably a matter of fashion. His slightly concave heater shield is slung on his back by its long guige. He is not riding his own destrier or war-horse while scouting in the forest, but has selected a smaller and perhaps more nimble local mount with a simple native Baltic or Finnish harness.

## H: SWEDISH ATTACK ON MUSCOVITE FORTRESS, 1496
In that year Swedish crusaders attacked the fortress of Ivangorod overlooking the River Narva on the eastern frontier of Estonia.

**H1: Swedish artilleryman**
By the late 15th century there had been many significant developments in European military equipment, in Scandinavia as elsewhere; not least was the widespread adoption of gunpowder weapons. Here an artilleryman prepares to fire a medium-sized cannon which is protected by a moveable timber shield. The firing is done by heating a touche in a charcoal brazier, then applying it to the touche hole' or touch hole. The gunner is protected by a notably bulbous style of brimmed chapel-de-fer that was very popular in Scandinavia. He also has a mail tippet on his neck and shoulders, and a long-sleeved, padded, and probably scale-lined jacque worn over a mail hauberk or haubergeon.

**H2: Finnish crossbowman**
In contrast to the lightly protected gunner, this crossbowman wears almost complete 'white harness' or fully plated armour. The only pieces that are missing are the massive breast and back plates with their attached hip-covering fauld.

Toompea Castle, the oldest part of the fortifications of the city of Reval, now called Tallinn, the capital of Estonia. See commentary Plate F. (D.Nicolle photograph)

The former have been replaced by a cloth-covered, scale-lined brigandine – in the case of a footsoldier, presumably for reasons of weight. His helmet is a particularly deep form of brimmed 'war-hat' with eye-slits cut in the front part of the brim. The crossbow is still of a relatively traditional form, but it is now spanned by means of the leverage exerted with an iron 'crow's-foot', which made it easier to pull back the strings of the more powerful forms of stave.

**H3: Swedish man-at-arms**
This man is clearly a member of the wealthy and fashion-conscious military elite. His helmet is of the latest style, an iron salet form with a visor that could be raised or lowered. This was often worn with a steel bevor which covered the chin, throat and upper chest; it did not move with the head, but was fixed to the breastplate. In addition to the loose tabbard which is fastened only at the shoulders, he has a velvet jacket with widely puffed sleeves. This garment goes over the armour of his arms, upper chest and back, but is tucked inside the plackart and fauld which protect his abdomen, hips and groin. Below this is a mail haubergeon. The leather sword belt is split so that one part goes closely around the waist of his armour while the other part falls loosely down to his left hip. The front of his hips have the additional protection of plated tassets, while the rest of his legs are enclosed in full steel leg harness.

# INDEX

References to illustrations are shown in **bold**. Plates are shown with page and caption locators in brackets.